GEO

W9-AGX-036

INSIDE THE NFL
AFC WEST

THE DENVER BRONCOS
THE KANSAS CITY CHIEFS
THE OAKLAND RAIDERS
THE SAN DIEGO CHARGERS

BY K. C. KELLEY

The Child's World

Published in the United States of America by
The Child's World® • 1980 Lookout Drive
Mankato, MN 56003-1705
800-599-READ • www.childsworld.com

ACKNOWLEDGEMENTS

The Child's World®: Mary Berendes,
Publishing Director

The Design Lab: Kathleen Petelinsek,
Design; Gregory Lindholm, Page Production

Manuscript consulting and photo research
by Shoreline Publishing Group LLC.

Thanks to John Walters and Jim Gigliotti for
their help with this book.

PHOTOS

Front cover: Joe Robbins
Back cover: Joe Robbins
Interior: AP/Wide World: 5, 10, 13, 14, 24, 26,
27, 31; Getty Images: 6;
Joe Robbins: 9, 12, 17, 19, 20, 23, 29, 32.

LIBRARY OF CONGRESS
CATALOGING-IN-PUBLICATION DATA

Kelley, K. C.
   AFC West / by K.C. Kelley.
      p. cm. — (Inside the NFL)
   Includes bibliographical references and index.
   ISBN 978-1-60253-004-1
(library bound : alk. paper)
   1. National Football League—History—Juvenile
literature. 2. Football—United States—History—
Juvenile literature. I. Title. II. Series.
   GV955.5.N35K449 2008
   796.332'640973—dc22   2008010522

AFC WEST
INTRODUCTION

All four of the teams in the AFC West have been champions at one time or another. Some won AFL titles, others won AFC titles, and three have won **Super Bowl** titles. From their first days in the old American Football League, these teams have often used some of the game's most exciting styles of play. They have also featured a host of outstanding talent as well as wild personalities.

The Broncos, the Chiefs (who were the Texans then), the Raiders, and the Chargers kicked off play together in 1960 in the AFL's first season. The AFL **merged** with the NFL in 1970, and the new AFC West went through several changes. However, as of 2006, when the NFL lined up into eight four-team divisions, the AFC West returned to its AFL roots. Since then, AFC West teams have been to the Super Bowl 13 times, winning six. Along with all those wins, they treated NFL fans to such moments as the "Heidi Game," the NFL's longest game, the "Immaculate Reception," and "The Drive," just to name a few. Let's take a trip to the "wild, wild West."

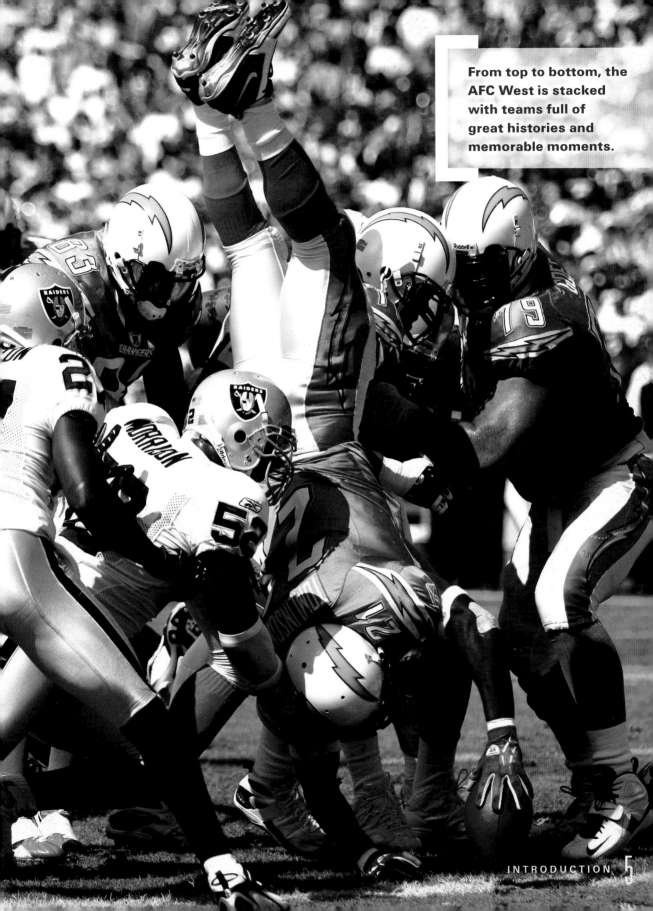

From top to bottom, the AFC West is stacked with teams full of great histories and memorable moments.

CHAPTER ONE
THE DENVER BRONCOS

F or the first 30-plus years of their existence, the Denver Broncos seemed as if they were playing horseshoes. They kept coming up just a bit short, achieving some good things, but never quite scoring a ringer—or should we say, a Super Bowl ring?

Things started well for the **franchise.** It was born in 1960, the first year of the new American Football League. The AFL was formed to compete with the older NFL. Eight teams started that first season. The Broncos were Colorado's first **professional** sports team and immediately became one of the hottest tickets in town.

On September 9, 1960, the league kicked off, with the Broncos winning the first AFL game. They beat the Boston (later New England) Patriots 13–10. After that hot start, however, it was pretty much all downhill. The Broncos would not have a winning season until 1973 and would not make the **playoffs** until 1977.

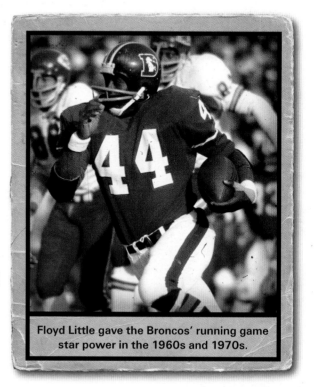

Floyd Little gave the Broncos' running game star power in the 1960s and 1970s.

One reason might have been their really ugly uniforms. Denver began play in chocolate-colored jerseys with gold helmets and pants. They wore socks with vertical stripes. After going 4–9–1 and 3–11 their first two seasons, the Broncos fired coach Frank Filchock. The new coach, Jack Faulkner, destroyed Denver's striped socks at a public bonfire and ordered dark, burnt-orange jerseys. The uniform maker delivered bright-orange jerseys by mistake. It turned out to be a good mistake, as the color defined the team for most of the next 30 years.

Wearing bright orange, Denver finished in last place in the AFL West each of the next five years. In the season-opening game in 1966, a 45–7 loss to the Houston Oilers, the Broncos failed to make a single first down. In 1968, Denver moved into newly enlarged and renamed Mile High Stadium, which would provide a huge home-field advantage over the next three decades. Why Mile High? The city of Denver is located more than 5,000 feet above sea level. There are 5,280 feet (1,609 m) in a mile! The air at that altitude is somewhat thinner, with less oxygen. Visiting teams can sometimes have trouble adjusting, while the hometown Broncos keep breathing easily.

In 1970, the AFL merged with the NFL. The Broncos were placed in the Western Division of the new American Football Conference. That year, halfback Floyd Little became the franchise's first star. He led the AFC in rushing with 901 yards. Denver won four of its first five games that year but finished the season just 5–8–1. Its bad luck continued for another six years.

The Broncos' fortunes changed in 1977, however. Craig Morton, the 26th starting quarterback in franchise history, led Denver to a 12–2 season. Finally, the Broncos were in the playoffs. Denver's vaunted "Orange Crush" defense (named after those bright jerseys as well as a popular soda) featured all-pros Lyle Alzado, Rubin Carter, Randy Gradishar, and Tom Jackson.

On Christmas Eve at Mile High Stadium, the Broncos won their first playoff game, humbling the Pittsburgh Steelers, 34–21. A week later, the Broncos edged the defending Super Bowl-champion Oakland Raiders, 20–17, earning a berth in Super Bowl XII. The long, cold years in Mile High paid off for enthusiastic fans. Their team would have a chance to win its first-ever NFL championship. Head coach Red Miller's team needed to play its best game to beat Dallas in the Super Bowl. Instead, the Broncos played their worst game of the season. Denver committed eight **turnovers** and lost 27–10.

In 1981, Dan Reeves was hired as head coach. Two years later, the Broncos made the biggest trade in franchise history when they acquired quarterback John Elway. The Stanford University quarterback had been made the number-one pick in the NFL **draft** by the Colts. Elway, the most famous **rookie** since the Jets' Joe Namath in 1965, had good looks, nimble feet, and a rifle arm. He would be Denver's star for the next 16 years.

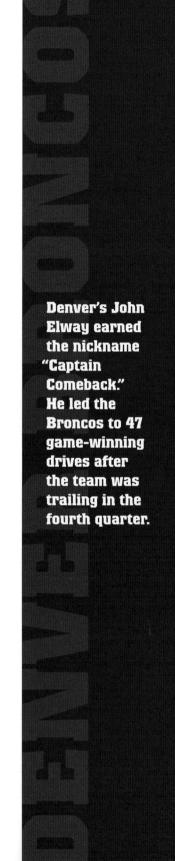

Denver's John Elway earned the nickname "Captain Comeback." He led the Broncos to 47 game-winning drives after the team was trailing in the fourth quarter.

Quarterback John Elway took the Broncos to five Super Bowls (winning two).

Elway led the Broncos to the playoffs his first two seasons. In his fourth year, he forged his legend with what is now simply known as "The Drive." Trailing 20–13 in frigid Cleveland in the AFC Championship Game, Elway marched the Broncos 98 yards in the final minutes for the game-tying touchdown. He completed short and long passes, made key runs, and managed the clock perfectly. With nine seconds left, he fired a five-yard touchdown pass to Mark Jackson to tie the score. Denver won in **overtime** on Rich Karlis's field goal. The game cemented Elway's **reputation** as one of the NFL's biggest stars.

The Broncos met the New York Giants in Super Bowl XXI in Pasadena. Again, the Broncos failed to win the big game. They lost 39–20. Unfortunately, a pattern was developing. The next year,

After many seasons of frustration, the Broncos took home the trophy as Super Bowl champs two years in a row (1997 and 1998).

Denver won the AFC championship again, only to lose to the Washington Redskins in Super Bowl XXII in San Diego, 42–10.

Two years later, Denver was off to its fourth Super Bowl, this time against a San Francisco 49ers team that was clearly superior. The Broncos were buried 55–10 in what was the most lopsided Super Bowl in history.

After a few average seasons, the Broncos returned to the Super Bowl in 1997 under third-year coach Mike Shanahan. Elway was still around and still finding ways to win. However, he didn't have to do it all himself this time around. He was finally teamed with a great running back in Terrell Davis, who gained 1,750 yards that year. All-pro tight end in Shannon Sharpe was a key target and an emotional leader. The trio helped Denver finally "win the big one," defeating the Green Bay Packers 31–24 in Super Bowl XXXII.

In 2005, Mike Shanahan became the winningest coach in Broncos' history. The offensive genius had racked up 138 wins through the 2007 season.

Not content with just one title, the Broncos were back in the Super Bowl the following year. Davis had another great season. He became just the fourth player ever to rush for 2,000 yards in a season, reaching a final total of 2,008. Sharpe was his usual amazing self, and Denver's defense was even better than the year before. This time, the Broncos beat former coach Reeves and his Atlanta Falcons, 34–19. Elway, playing in his final game, was named MVP. He rode off the field in triumph as one of the greatest players in football history.

Since then, the Broncos have searched for a **successor** to Elway. Brian Griese, the son of Hall of Fame quarterback Bob Griese, was the first to fill Elway's shoes. But after Denver missed the playoffs three times in the four years immediately following Elway's **retirement,** the Broncos signed **free-agent** quarterback Jake Plummer in 2003. Plummer helped lead Denver to back-to-back 10-win seasons and a **wild-card** spot in the playoffs each of his first two seasons with the club.

Injuries forced Davis into retirement, too, so the Broncos turned to Clinton Portis in 2002. He had one of the NFL's best rookie seasons ever in 2002, running for 1,508 yards, and then he added 1,591 yards the next year. But Denver, desperate for help on the defensive side of the ball, traded him to Washington for star cornerback Champ Bailey before the 2004 season.

Good running backs keep turning up in Denver, however. Part of the reason is Shanahan's reliance on a solid run game. The team has had

The Broncos hope that current quarterback Jay Cutler can follow in John Elway's legendary footsteps.

a 1,000-yard rusher nearly every season he's been their coach. In 2006, it was a pair of running bells that took over and rang in a playoff spot for Denver. Mike Bell topped 1,000 yards and Tatum Bell led the team with eight touchdowns. Along with Plummer, they led the Broncos all the way to a 13–3 mark and a spot in the AFC Championship Game. Though they lost there to Pittsburgh, it was one of the best seasons in recent Broncos' history.

After Mike Anderson took over the revolving running back spot in 2006, Travis Henry led the way in 2007. Another young star trying to get the Broncos back to the playoffs is quarterback Jay Cutler. The first-round draft pick in 2006 took over from Plummer as the team's starter late in his rookie year. By 2007, he was "the man" in Denver, and showed off his strong arm with 20 touchdown passes. With the wily Shanahan still roaming the sidelines and a long tradition of success, look for Denver to be back among the top teams in the coming seasons.

CHAPTER TWO
THE KANSAS CITY CHIEFS

The most important person in Kansas City Chiefs' history never put on a helmet or called a play. All Lamar Hunt did was own, build, and lead. Hunt was the founder and longtime owner of the Chiefs. He and seven other members of the "Foolish Club" decided to start the American Football League (AFL) in 1960. Hunt had tried to buy and NFL team but was unsuccessful . . . so he started his own pro league!

At first, his team played in Dallas as the Texans, but moved to Kansas City in 1963 and took its current name. While in Dallas, however, the club did pretty well, winning the 1962 AFL championship. The title game was a classic. The Texans and Houston Oilers were tied 17–17 at the end of regulation. After 77 minutes and 54 seconds—the longest game in pro football history at the time—Dallas won when Tommy Brooker kicked a field goal.

Coach Hank Stram was on top of the world after the Chiefs won Super Bowl IV.

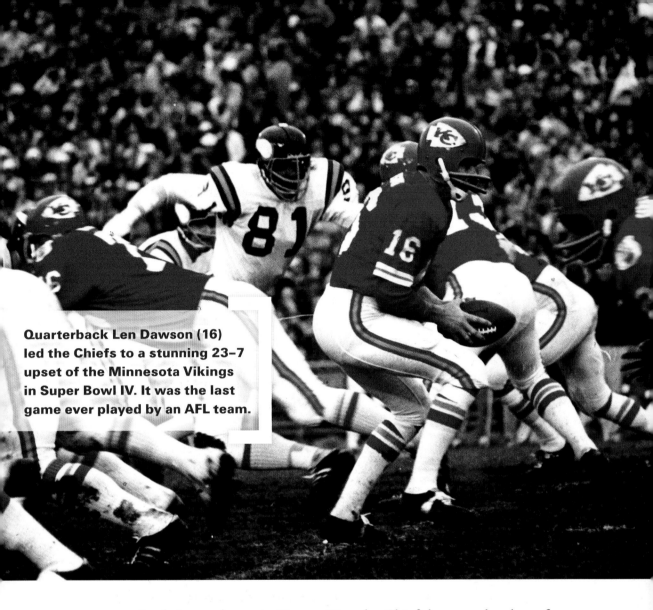

Quarterback Len Dawson (16) led the Chiefs to a stunning 23–7 upset of the Minnesota Vikings in Super Bowl IV. It was the last game ever played by an AFL team.

In their new home in Kansas City, the Chiefs became the class of the AFL. They sported a brilliant coach, Hank Stram, and a terrific quarterback in Len Dawson. In 1966, Dawson led the AFL with 26 touchdown passes. His favorite target was Otis Taylor, a tall, physical receiver who averaged a league-best 22.4 yards per catch. Kansas City won its second AFL championship that year, easily beating the Buffalo Bills in the title game, 31–7.

That season, the AFL and NFL champions played each other for the first time in the AFL-NFL World Championship Game. It is now

Len Dawson was a Hall of Fame quarterback for Kansas City. But he holds one record he's probably not proud of. His seven fumbles in one 1964 game remains a single-game record.

known as the Super Bowl. That first game matched the Chiefs against the NFL's Green Bay Packers. The two teams met at the Los Angeles Coliseum on January 15, 1967. Kansas City trailed 14–10 at halftime, putting a bit of a scare into the mighty NFL champs. However, Kansas City fell apart in the second half and lost 35–10.

Two seasons later, the Chiefs relied on their defense to post a 12–2 record. They featured future Hall of Famers such as nose tackle Curley Culp, defensive tackle Buck Buchanan, and linebackers Bobby Bell and Willie Lanier. Together, they allowed an AFL record-low 170 points all season. The Chiefs lost in the playoffs, though, to the Oakland Raiders.

In 1969, Kansas City put it all together. Again, the rugged defense allowed the fewest points (177) in the league. The Chiefs finished 11–3, second to Oakland in the AFL West. In the playoffs, they beat the defending Super Bowl-champion New York Jets, 13–6. In that game, the defense staged a famous goal-line stand. It rose up to stop the Jets on three straight plays inside the one-yard line. The following weekend, the Chiefs beat Oakland 17–7 in the AFL title game. Kansas City then won its first and only Super Bowl. Dawson led the Chiefs to a 23–7 victory over the Minnesota Vikings in Super Bowl IV. After that season, the two leagues became one, and the Chiefs joined the new American Football Conference's West division.

In 1971, the Chiefs won the AFC West with a 10–3–1 record. On Christmas Day 1971, they hosted the Miami Dolphins in an AFC Divisional Playoff Game. The game not only went into overtime, but it became the longest game in NFL history. Miami won 27–24 when Garo Yepremian kicked the winning field goal in the game's 83rd minute.

Except for the team's move into Arrowhead Stadium in 1972, the rest of the 1970s was forgettable. After 1973, Kansas City would not have another winning season until 1981.

In 1986, the Chiefs returned to the playoffs for the first time in 15 years. They lost their **postseason** opener to the Jets, though, 35–15. In 1989, super-sized Christian Okoye, also known as the "Nigerian Nightmare," became the league's most feared rusher. Okoye steamrollered defenders en route to an NFL-best 1,480 rushing yards.

The Chiefs returned to the playoffs in 1990, spearheaded by an outstanding defense. End Neil Smith and linebacker Derrick Thomas led a unit that accounted for 60 **sacks** and 45 turnovers. Thomas had 20 sacks, including an NFL-record seven in one game. Kansas City lost in the first round to Miami, however.

Under coach Marty Schottenheimer, the Chiefs would return to the playoffs each of the next five years. They never made it back to the Super Bowl, though. The toughest season was 1995, when Kansas City finished with a league-best 13–3 record. But the Chiefs were upset by Indianapolis in the playoffs. Kansas City was 13–3 again in 1997, only to lose to the Broncos in the playoffs.

In a 1971 playoff loss to Miami, running back Ed Podolak piled up 350 combined yards (rushing, receiving, and kick returns). This postseason record still stands.

Larry Johnson is the latest in a line of Chiefs' rushing stars. He set a club record when he gained 1,789 yards in 2006.

In January 2000, the Chiefs were devastated when Thomas—Kansas City's best and most popular player—died of injuries he suffered in a car accident.

The Chiefs eventually missed the playoffs for the fourth **consecutive** year the following season, but in 2001 Kansas City's hopes were restored by the hiring of Dick Vermeil as head coach.

Vermeil, who had been out of coaching for one season after leading the St. Louis Rams to victory in Super Bowl XXXIV, immediately began molding the Chiefs into a **contender.**

By 2002, he had built the NFL's highest-scoring offense around star running back Priest Holmes, quarterback Trent Green, and tight end Tony Gonzalez. One year later, the Chiefs won 13 regular-season games and the AFC West title, and reached the playoffs for the first time since the 1997 season. They averaged 30.3 points per game that year while scoring 484 points, the most in the NFL.

In 2004, the Chiefs kept up the scoring, posting 40 or more points in four games. However, they didn't spread their points around as well, finishing 7–9. A 10–6 record in 2005 was pretty good, but not good enough to earn a playoff spot. Larry Johnson emerged as one of the NFL's top running backs, piling up 1,750 yards and scoring 20 touchdowns. Kansas City won nine games under new coach Herm Edwards in 2006, as Johnson ran for 1,789 yards and 17 touchdowns. The Chiefs did make the playoffs that season, but lost to the eventual Super Bowl champion, the Indianapolis Colts.

Off those two winning years, the 2007 season got off to a good start. The Chiefs were 4–2 and playing great. Damon Huard was effective at quarterback, while Gonzalez was on the way to his best season yet. However, the team's **bye week**— and an injury to Johnson—shut them down. Following their week off, the Chiefs lost nine straight games, wrapping up one of their worst years. They're hoping that taking seven months off didn't do the same thing for their 2008 season!

Chiefs running back Priest Holmes set an NFL record with 27 touchdowns in 2003. However, his mark has since been topped by Shaun Alexander (28 in 2005) and LaDainian Tomlinson (31 in 2006).

Tony Gonzalez is one of the best pass-catching tight ends in the history of the NFL.

CHAPTER THREE

THE OAKLAND RAIDERS

ith a skull-and-crossbones as their logo and silver and black for colors, the Raiders have built a decades-long style of scaring opponents. However, in recent years, their play hasn't been frightening . . . it's just been scary. Scary for their own fans to watch, that is. The team built a long record of success, including titles in both the AFL and the Super Bowl. However, since reaching the AFC Championship Game in 2002, the Raiders have fallen on hard times.

The Silver and Black, as the Raiders are often called after their team colors, was founded in 1960. They were one of the original eight AFL teams. They didn't have much success at first, losing 19 in a row at one point in 1961 and 1962. Before the 1963 season, however, the Raiders'

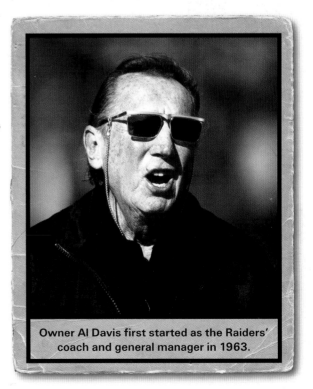

Owner Al Davis first started as the Raiders' coach and general manager in 1963.

fortunes—and NFL history—changed forever. Oakland hired Al Davis, a young assistant coach with the San Diego Chargers, as its head coach and general manager. "We started doing things first class instead of third class," said former Raiders center Jim Otto.

Over the next 40-plus years, Davis would become the person most identified with one team. He would lead the Raiders on and off the field, first as coach and later as the owner. Nothing happened on the Raiders without Davis' okay. His all-black or all-white sweatsuits and dark sunglasses became well-known throughout the sports world. His motto of "Just win, baby!" would become more famous than many of his players.

In his early years with the club, Davis began building the kind of loyalty among players that helped him create great Raiders teams. Center Jim Otto, who famously wore number 00, was a fixture on the offensive line for the franchise's first 15 seasons. Wide receiver Fred Biletnikoff was a star for years and later a longtime Raiders coach. Quarterback and kicker George Blanda played until his late 40s.

Led by Davis, Oakland went 13–1 in 1967. Quarterback Daryle Lamonica was the AFL's most valuable player, and the Raiders crushed the Houston Oilers 40–7 in the AFL Championship Game. Oakland met the Green Bay Packers in Super Bowl II, but lost 33–14.

In 1968, the Raiders were involved in one of the most famous games in NFL history. Oakland trailed the visiting New York Jets 32–29 with just more than a minute to play in a nationally televised game. Suddenly, the clock struck 7 P.M. NBC switched from the game to its regularly scheduled program, the film *Heidi*. Thousands of angry football fans called to complain. They all missed an amazing ending to a wild game. In the final minute, Oakland scored a pair of touchdowns to win, 43–32.

Four years later, Oakland, then coached by John Madden, visited the Pittsburgh Steelers in a divisional playoff game. The contest was decided by one of the most famous plays in NFL history, the "Immaculate Reception."

Only 22 seconds remained. Oakland led 7–6. Pittsburgh faced fourth down and 10 with the ball on its own 40. Steelers quarterback Terry Bradshaw heaved a pass to running back Frenchy Fuqua. Raiders safety Jack Tatum collided with Fuqua as the ball arrived. The football ricocheted into the arms of Steelers running back Franco Harris. Harris caught the ball just above his shoelaces and rambled 42 yards for the winning touchdown. It was a stunning loss, but the Raiders bounced back.

In 1976, the Raiders won the AFC West for the ninth time in 10 seasons. Their 13–1 squad was filled with free-spirited legends. Four players from the team would eventually make the Pro Football Hall of Fame. They included tight end Dave Casper and Biletnikoff. Others on their way to the Hall were offensive linemen Art Shell, who was a tackle, and Gene Upshaw, who was a guard.

The Raiders' Tom Flores was the first Hispanic head coach in the NFL. The former quarterback coached the Raiders from 1979 to 1987 and led them to two Super Bowls.

Running back Marcus Allen always had a nose for the end zone.

Oakland, which had lost the last three AFC Championship Games, finally made it back to the Super Bowl by squashing Pittsburgh in the conference title game. Then the Silver and Black manhandled the Minnesota Vikings 32–14 in Super Bowl XI. Al Davis finally had his NFL title.

In 1978, the Raiders forced an NFL rule change following a 21–20 win at San Diego. Oakland trailed 20–14 in the final seconds. The play was typical of the "Just win, baby!" spirit of Davis and the Raiders. A moment before being sacked, Stabler purposely fumbled the ball forward. Another player intentionally batted the ball toward the end zone. Casper fell on it there for the game-winning touchdown. After that, the league added a new rule. Now, only the player who fumbles the ball on fourth down or in the final two minutes can advance it.

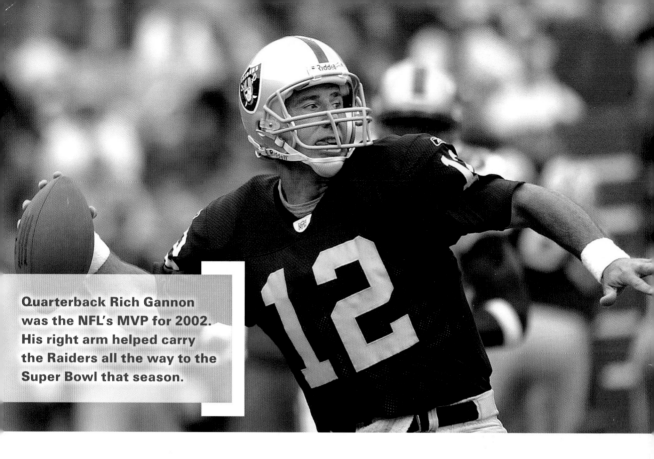

Madden retired after the 1978 season and launched a career as a top football TV announcer and video-game spokesman. However, the Raiders remained successful. Quarterback Jim Plunkett, a former **Heisman Trophy** winner, was the MVP of Oakland's 27–10 victory over Philadelphia in Super Bowl XV to cap the 1980 season. Three years later, running back Marcus Allen, another former Heisman Trophy winner, led the Raiders to a 38–9 rout of Washington in Super Bowl XVIII.

By that time, the Raiders were in Los Angeles. In 1982, Davis had moved the team. The always-tough Davis had argued with the city of Oakland about the team's home there. Ignoring threats from the NFL and Oakland, Davis made the move to southern California. The Raiders remained there for 13 seasons. The highlights of the Los Angeles era included the hiring of Art Shell as head coach in 1989. The former tackle became the NFL's first African-American head coach since Fritz Pollard in 1920.

Following another dispute, this time with folks in Los Angeles, the Raiders returned to Oakland in 1995. (Don't worry, he was still arguing with Oakland's people, too!) In the 2001 postseason, the Raiders lost a heartbreaking divisional playoff game at New England. Patriots quarterback Tom Brady appeared to lose a fumble late in the game, clinching the win for Oakland. The officials overruled themselves in the snowy night, however. Their ruling gave New England another chance. The Patriots eventually won the game and, two weeks later, Super Bowl XXXVI.

In 2002, the Raiders returned to AFC supremacy. They finished with the conference's best record at 11–5. Veteran quarterback Rich Gannon was the league's MVP. He guided a powerful offense that also featured two of the most **prolific** wide receivers in NFL history: longtime Raiders player Tim Brown and former San Francisco 49ers star Jerry Rice. In the playoffs, Oakland easily beat the Jets and the Titans to win the conference title. Though the Raiders lost Super Bowl XXXVII to the Buccaneers, the Silver and Black had proved it was back.

Not for long. One year after winning the AFC championship, Oakland tumbled to a 4–12 mark in 2003 (equaling the poorest in the NFL). It was one of the biggest one-season drops in league history. Head coach Bill Callahan was replaced by Norv Turner the following season, but the Raiders' fortunes improved only slightly. They won only five games and finished in last place in the AFC West.

The Raiders hope that young JaMarcus Russell (2) is the man who can return the club to its past glory.

One bright spot was the play of quarterback Kerry Collins, a free agent. Collins, the man who helped lead the New York Giants to Super Bowl XXXV in the 2000 season, replaced the injured Gannon early in the year. Despite starting only 13 games, he passed for 3,495 yards and 21 touchdowns.

That record of 4–12 proved to be a sticking point for the Raiders. That was their record in 2004, 2005, and 2007. What happened in 2006? That was even worse, as they finished 2–14, including being shut out three times and held below 10 points in four other games. Where did all the offense go?

Those low finishes gave the Raiders some good draft picks, and their fans hope the number-one choice in 2007, JaMarcus Russell, can be the quarterback to lead them back to the top. But the team faced a lot of uncertainty going into 2008. The future for the Raiders is cloudy.

CHAPTER FOUR
THE SAN DIEGO CHARGERS

For most of their history, the Chargers were known for their lightning-like **aerial** abilities, with a series of top passers and receivers shattering records. However, in recent years, they have been carried to the playoffs several times on the powerful legs of one of the top running backs in NFL history.

Lightning first struck in Los Angeles, not San Diego. The Chargers started play in 1960 in L.A. as one of the original members of the American Football League (AFL). For the first half of the 1960s, they were one of pro football's most successful teams, reaching the AFL Championship Game five times.

Sid Gillman, who is to the exciting offense what Thomas Edison was to the light bulb, was the Chargers' first coach. Talk about electric: On the team's first play in its first preseason game, Paul Lowe returned a kickoff 105 yards for a touchdown.

Head coach Sid Gillman was a mastermind on offense.

The Chargers won the AFL West their first year, 1960, with a 10–4 record. They averaged 26.6 points per game. Quarterback Jack Kemp, an NFL reject, was rated the league's best passer. In the first AFL Championship Game, Los Angeles lost 24–16 to the Houston Oilers.

The following season, the Chargers moved to San Diego. They went 12–2 but again lost to Houston in the championship game.

After their first losing season in 1962, San Diego made three straight trips to the AFL Championship Game. In 1963, the Chargers beat the Boston Patriots 51–10 to win their first, and only, title. They lost the championship game to the Buffalo Bills in each of the next two seasons. Adding insult to injury, the quarterback of those Bills' squads was Kemp. The Chargers had tried to sneak Kemp through **waivers** during the 1962 preseason. Buffalo claimed him for $100.

Lance Alworth was the Chargers' star. Nicknamed "Bambi" because of his thin build and quickness, Alworth averaged 100 receiving yards per game for three straight seasons beginning in 1964. Alworth's sure hands and ability to escape tackles made him unforgettable. In 1978, he became the first AFL player enshrined in the Pro Football Hall of Fame.

Alworth's spot in the Hall must have energized the Chargers. The franchise had failed to finish better than third place from 1966 to 1978, but suddenly San Diego's offense reacted as if it had been struck by lightning. Actually, the fire-starter

Pro Football Hall of Fame quarterback Johnny Unitas finished the last season of his great career with San Diego in 1973.

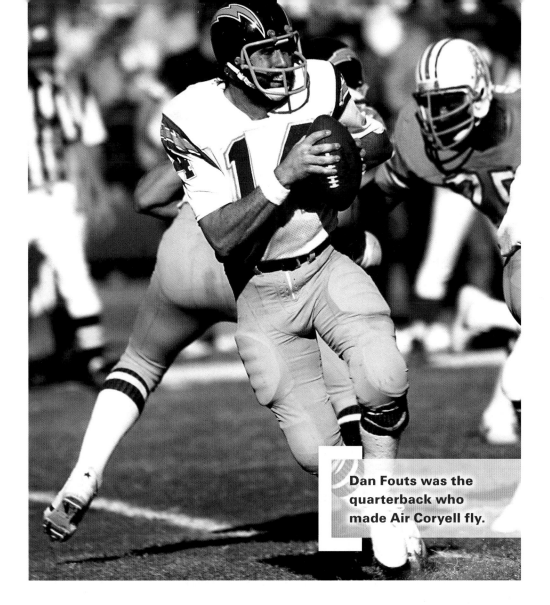

Dan Fouts was the quarterback who made Air Coryell fly.

was head coach Don Coryell, who was hired in 1978. Coryell had the most inventive offensive mind pro football had seen since Gillman.

The new coach's offense was known as "Air Coryell." His primary weapons were quarterback Dan Fouts and tight end Kellen Winslow, who were both future Hall of Famers. Wide receivers John Jefferson and Charlie Joiner, also a Hall of Famer, played big parts, too.

In 1979, Fouts had four consecutive 300-yard games (a record) and passed for 4,082 yards (another record). At 12–4, the Chargers were not only winners, but they were also tremendous fun to watch.

San Diego lost its playoff opener in 1979 to Houston, 17–14. But Air Coryell returned in 1980 and soared even higher. Fouts passed for 4,715 yards and his trio of receivers each had 1,000-yard seasons. The Chargers beat Buffalo 20–14 in the first round of the playoffs for their first postseason victory since 1963. The following weekend, San Diego lost 34–27 to Oakland in the AFC Championship Game.

In 1981, the Chargers won the AFC West for the third straight year. Fouts again shattered the passing yardage barrier with 4,802. Winslow led the AFC in receptions for the second year in a row. It was all a preview before one of the most memorable postseason games ever.

On January 2, 1982, the Chargers traveled to Miami to face the Dolphins in a divisional playoff. San Diego led 24–0 after one quarter. But Miami came back, and the teams were tied 38–38 after four quarters. In overtime, Winslow blocked a field-goal try. Finally, after 13:52 of overtime, the Chargers' Rolf Benirschke made the game-winning field goal.

The Chargers' glory was short-lived. Eight days later, the temperature in Cincinnati was 11 degrees below zero, a far cry from the balmy weather in San Diego. The Chargers lost 27–7, and they would not return to the playoffs for 10 years.

The drought ended in 1992. The new-look Chargers relied on defensive stoppers such as end Leslie O'Neal and linebacker Junior Seau (pronounced "Say Ow!") to win the AFC West.

In 1995, punter Darren Bennett joined the Chargers. He became the first Australian-born player to reach the Pro Bowl, which is the NFL's yearly all-star game.

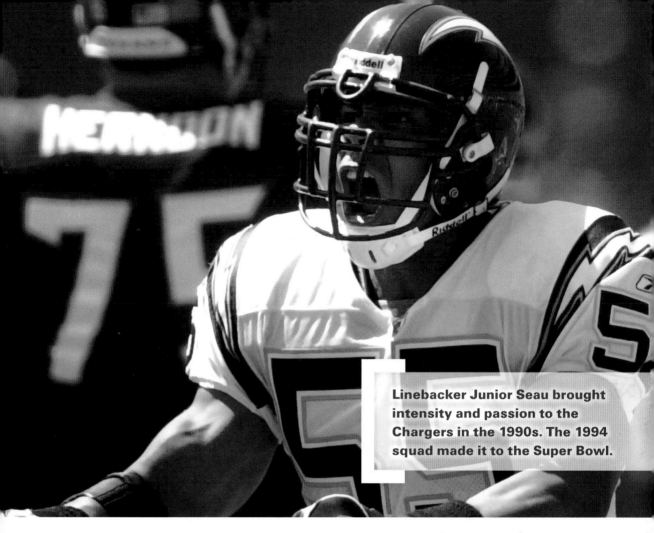

Linebacker Junior Seau brought intensity and passion to the Chargers in the 1990s. The 1994 squad made it to the Super Bowl.

Two years later, the Chargers advanced all the way to the Super Bowl. Burly fullback Natrone Means gained a franchise-record 1,350 yards. Head coach Bobby Ross put together a defense that stuffed opponents—that is, until Super Bowl XXIX. The San Francisco 49ers won that game easily, 49–26.

Ross left a few seasons later. For a while, the Chargers played terribly and lost a lot of games. In fact, in 2000, San Diego tied an NFL record by losing 15 games.

The silver lining to that dark cloud, however, came in the 2001 draft. Because the Chargers had the league's poorest record, they owned the top selection. Superstar quarterback Michael Vick was available, but San Diego traded the choice. And though the Chargers

LaDainian Tomlinson is both a rushing and receiving threat. He has become one of the greatest superstars of the 2000s—and maybe ever.

were criticized for the move, it let them to come away with two excellent players instead of one: quarterback Drew Brees and running back LaDainian Tomlinson, known as "LT."

Tomlinson was an immediate star. He set a franchise record by running for 1,683 yards in 2002. The next year, he set another record by catching 100 passes. Brees took a little longer to develop, but he had a breakout season in 2004, when he passed for 3,159 yards and 27 touchdowns.

That year, San Diego won 12 games and made the playoffs for the first time since 1995. Brees was named the NFL's comeback player of the year (he had passed for just 2,108 yards and 11 touchdowns the season before). Marty Schottenheimer, who had been hired in 2002, was named the coach of the year. However, that season ended with a heartbreaking loss to the New York Jets in overtime in the first round of the playoffs.

After missing the postseason in 2004 and 2005, the Chargers, now quarterbacked by Philip Rivers, made it again in 2006, thanks to a monster year from LT. He scored an amazing 31 touchdowns, breaking the league mark by three. His total of 186 points was also a league-best, topping a record set way back in 1962. He led San Diego to the playoffs, but even his 123 yards weren't enough to stop quarterback Tom Brady and the Patriots.

In 2007, San Diego welcomed a new coach, Norv Turner, in an effort to turn regular-season success into playoff punch. Turner did just that. After starting the season 1–3, the Chargers charged into the playoffs playing their best football of the year. LT led the league in rushing, while tight end Antonio Gates had another tremendous season. San Diego beat Tennessee in the first round. Then the Chargers faced the defending Super Bowl-champion Colts, who were 13–3, in the next round. And even though both LT and Rivers missed the fourth quarter with injuries, San Diego rallied to upset Indianapolis 28–24.

In the AFC Championship Game, the Chargers ran into the New England Patriots' undefeated machine. With LT injured and out for most of the game, the Chargers didn't have a chance. But with its collection of young stars, San Diego figures to have more than a chance in the years ahead.

In 2004, Antonio Gates set an NFL record for tight ends by catching 13 touchdown passes.

TIME LINE

1960
The Dallas Texans, Denver Broncos, Los Angeles Chargers, and Oakland Raiders become charter members of the American Football League

1969
Chiefs win the last Super Bowl before the AFL-NFL merger, beating Minnesota

1976
Raiders beat the Vikings for the first of the franchise's three Super Bowl victories

1977
Denver makes the playoffs for the first time in franchise history but loses Super Bowl XI to Dallas

1960 | 1970 | 1980

1980
Raiders beat Philadelphia to win Super Bowl XV

1966
San Diego wins its first, and only, league championship

1982
Oakland shifts its franchise to Los Angeles

1963
Texans move to Kansas City and become the Chiefs

1961
Chargers move their franchise to San Diego

1983
In their second year in Los Angeles, the Raiders rout Washington to win Super Bowl XVIII

1986
Denver wins first of three AFC championships in four-year span

1994
San Diego reaches the Super Bowl for the first time, but loses game XXIX to San Francisco

1995
Raiders move back to Oakland

1997
After four losses in the Super Bowl, the Broncos win the first of back-to-back titles

1990　　　2000　　　2010

2002
Raiders reach the Super Bowl for the first time in 19 seasons, but lose game XXXVII to Tampa Bay

2006
Chargers win an NFL-best (and franchise-record) 14 games during the regular season, but fall in their opening playoff game

2007
Chargers reach the AFC Championship Game before losing to New England

STAT STUFF

TEAM RECORDS (THROUGH 2007)*

Team	All-time Record	Number of Titles (Most Recent)	Number of Times in Playoffs	Top Coach (Wins)
Denver	395–351–10	2 (1998)	17	Mike Shanahan (138)
Kansas City	387–346–12	2 (1969)	15	Hank Stram (129)
Oakland	425–331–11	4 (1983)	21	John Madden (112)
San Diego	363–373–11	1 (1963)	15	Sid Gillman (83)

*includes AFL and NFL totals

AFC WEST CAREER LEADERS (THROUGH 2007)

Category	Name (Years With Team)	Total
Denver		
Rushing yards	Terrell Davis (1995–2002)	7,607
Passing yards	John Elway (1983–1998)	51,475
Touchdown passes	John Elway (1983–1998)	300
Receptions	Rod Smith (1995–2007)	849
Touchdowns	Rod Smith (1995–2007)	69
Scoring	Jason Elam (1993–2007)	1,786
Kansas City		
Rushing yards	Priest Holmes (2001–05, 2007)	6,070
Passing yards	Len Dawson (1962–1975)	28,507
Touchdown passes	Len Dawson (1962–1975)	237
Receptions	Tony Gonzalez (1997–2007)	820
Touchdowns	Priest Holmes (2001–05, 2007)	83
Scoring	Nick Lowery (1980–1993)	1,466
Oakland		
Rushing yards	Marcus Allen (1982–1992)	8,545
Passing yards	Ken Stabler (1970–79)	19,078
Touchdown passes	Ken Stabler (1970–79)	150
Receptions	Tim Brown (1988–2003)	1,070
Touchdowns	Tim Brown (1988–2003)	104
Scoring	George Blanda (1967–1975)	863
San Diego		
Rushing yards	LaDainian Tomlinson (2001–07)	10,650
Passing yards	Dan Fouts (1973–1987)	43,040
Touchdown passes	Dan Fouts (1973–1987)	254
Receptions	Charlie Joiner (1976–1986)	586
Touchdowns	LaDainian Tomlinson (2001–07)	129
Scoring	John Carney (1990–2000)	1,076

Player	Position	Date Inducted
Denver		
Willie Brown	Cornerback	1984
Tony Dorsett	Running Back	1994
John Elway	Quarterback	2004
Gary Zimmerman	Tackle	2008
Kansas City		
Marcus Allen	Running Back	2003
Bobby Bell	Linebacker/Defensive End	1983
Junious "Buck" Buchanan	Defensive Tackle	1990
Len Dawson	Quarterback	1987
Lamar Hunt	Owner	1972
Willie Lanier	Linebacker	1986
Marv Levy	Coach	2001
Joe Montana	Quarterback	2002
Warren Moon	Quarterback	2006
Jan Stenerud	Kicker	1991
Hank Stram	Coach	2003
Emmitt Thomas	Cornerback	2008
Mike Webster	Center	1997
Oakland		
Marcus Allen	Running Back	2003
Fred Biletnikoff	Wide Receiver	1988
George Blanda	Quarterback/Kicker	1981
Bob "Boomer" Brown	Tackle	2004
Willie Brown	Cornerback	1984
Dave Casper	Tight End	2002
Al Davis	Owner/Coach	1992
Eric Dickerson	Running Back	1999
Mike Haynes	Cornerback	1997
Ted Hendricks	Linebacker	1990
James Lofton	Wide Receiver	2003
Howie Long	Defensive End	2000
Ronnie Lott	Cornerback/Safety	2000
John Madden	Coach	2006
Ron Mix	Tackle	1979
Jim Otto	Center	1980
Art Shell	Tackle	1989
Gene Upshaw	Guard	1987
San Diego		
Lance Alworth	Flanker	1978
Fred Dean	Defensive End	2008
Dan Fouts	Quarterback	1993
Sid Gillman	Coach	1983
Charlie Joiner	Wide Receiver	1996
David "Deacon" Jones	Defensive End	1980
Larry Little	Guard	1993
John Mackey	Tight End	1992
Ron Mix	Tackle	1979
Johnny Unitas	Quarterback	1979
Kellen Winslow	Tight End	1995

GLOSSARY

aerial—having to do with the air; in this case, that means passing the football

bye week—a week during the season in which a team does not have a game scheduled

consecutive—in a row; one after the other

contender—a team with a good chance for a championship

draft—held each April, this is when NFL teams choose college players to join their teams; the teams with the worst records the prior season choose first, but draft picks can be traded to move a team's draft order

franchise—more than just the team, it is the entire organization that is a member of a professional sports league

free agent—a player who is not signed with a team

fumbles—when a ballcarrier drops the football during a play

Heisman Trophy—the award presented each year to the best player in college football

interceptions—passes that are caught by the defense instead of the offense

merged—joined together

overtime—the period of a game played if the score is tied after 60 minutes

playoffs—after the regular schedule, these are the games played to determine the champion

postseason—the period in which the playoffs are held

professional—taking part in a sport for pay

prolific—very productive

reputation—what other people think about someone else

retirement—the time after a person leaves a career for good

rookie—an athlete in his or her first season as a professional

sacks—when quarterbacks are tackled behind the line of scrimmage while attempting to pass

successor—a person who takes over someone else's job

Super Bowl—the NFL's championship game, played in late January or early February at a different stadium each year

turnovers—when teams give up possession of the ball by throwing interceptions or losing fumbles

waivers—when teams give up their rights to players, allowing other teams to sign them

wild-card—a team that makes the playoffs without winning a division title

FIND OUT MORE

Books

Ellenport, Craig. *LaDainian Tomlinson: All-Pro On and Off the Field*. Berkeley Heights, N.J.: Enslow Publishers, Inc., 2007.

Frisch, Aaron. *The History of the Oakland Raiders*. Mankato, Minn.: Creative Education, 2005.

Gonzalez, Tony, and Greg Brown. *Tony Gonzalez: Catch and Connect*. Kirkland, Wash.: Positively for Kids, 2004.

Hawkes, Brian. *The History of the Kansas City Chiefs*. Mankato, Minn.: Creative Education, 2005.

Ladewski, Paul. *National Football League Superstars 2007*. New York: Scholastic, 2007.

Marini, Matt. *Football Top 10*. New York: DK Publishing, 2002.

Schmalzbauer, Adam. *The History of the Denver Broncos*. Mankato, Minn.: Creative Education, 2004.

Schmalzbauer, Adam. *The History of the San Diego Chargers*. Mankato, Minn.: Creative Education, 2005.

On the Web

Visit our Web site for lots of links about the AFC West: *http://www.childsworld.com/links*

Note to Parents, Teachers, and Librarians: We routinely verify our Web links to make sure they are safe, active sites—so encourage your readers to check them out!

INDEX